BLUE
HIMALAYAN
POPPIES

BLUE HIMALAYAN POPPIES

Jay Ruzesky

NIGHTWOOD EDITIONS

Copyright © 2001 by Jay Ruzesky

Nightwood Editions
R.R. #22, 3692 Beach Avenue
Roberts Creek, BC
Canada V0N 2W2

Printed and bound in Canada

THE CANADA COUNCIL | LE CONSEIL DES ARTS
FOR THE ARTS | DU CANADA
SINCE 1957 | DEPUIS 1957

Nightwood Editions acknowledges the financial support of the Government
of Canada through the Book Publishing Industry Development Program
(BPIDP) and the Canada Council for the Arts, and the Province of British
Columbia through the British Columbia Arts Council, for its publishing
activities.

Edited for the house by Silas White

National Library of Canada Cataloguing in Publication Data

Ruzesky, Jay, 1965–
   Blue Himalayan poppies

   Poems.
   ISBN 0-88971-176-3

   I. Title.
PS8585.U99B58 2001   C811'.54   C2001-911299-8
PR9199.3.R87B58 2001

TABLE OF CONTENTS

*. . . and if I repent of any thing,
it is very likely to be my good behaviour.*

– Thoreau, *Walden*

LONG BEACH

My friend who doesn't smoke
speaks with a gravel voice the river
has rolled over.

Those stones, they've earned their patience.

He is quoting Stevie Smith:
"I was much farther out than you thought
And not waving but drowning."
His eyes wrinkle.

At Long Beach it is possible to believe
the sea is the unconscious.
There is that much to say.

Two men, each having taken a lover,
talk through miles of footprints
of what it is
to stand looking out the window
into a backyard at midnight, a wife
knotted in bed wondering if
he'll be coming in again.

Sand under their feet is hourglass impatient.

The ocean is big enough to wake from.

All day we ride body-boards
pressing them down on
edges of waves before they hit the beach.
He slides across the surface
imitating a star-cruiser in a space movie.

We bob in the afternoon,
black-hooded buoys,
the current sucking our feet
as waves undermine themselves;
the way wholeness is swamped just
when you think you're getting somewhere.

There is a moment when we realize
we are moving too quickly with the riptide,
can no longer touch bottom.

We have been saved
by a seventh wave – a big one that washed us
back to footholds.
We can laugh about it now over
drinks from our bottle of Irish.
We are cooking tortillas,
talking about how long it would have taken
to float to Japan.

He, at least, knows the language.

After dinner we are on the beach again,
the bonfire snapping like bones,
a big bottle of red wine.
We sing off-key and a little drunkenly.
Tomorrow we will go back.

The moon is a crescent turning away from us
and if the moon dreams, it dreams of speaking.

LENDING LIBRARY

When did my wife loan
my copy of *The Gold Cell*
for a friend's English paper?

This morning I found a renegade inscription
standing out the way painted initials
startle on rock faces in National Parks.
It was signed "with all my love."
At first I thought I had a secret admirer.

Imagine her, the friend, late at night
bent into November deadlines
at a desk lit by a small
green lamp. It is late and she
is tired, but drawn in by
the animal of sex roaming
the body from birth
looking for its own way out, pushing up
against parts of the skin
whenever someone touched there.
As she leans into words like *pod*,
rivulets, and *introductory cough*
her long hair writes across the bottom of a page
until the border between who she is
and what the poet has written
is no longer clear. She will read and reread
until the man sets a hand
on her shoulder and says it is time

for bed, and when he touches her
the skin that his hand has inhabited
will feel that small animal aching
toward his blood, and then his own longing,
a sudden promise, will head for his cock
and he will set his hands lower on her body,
lift her from the chair.
She will take his hand and lead.

This morning I opened the book
expecting to see old friends
but instead found
"For S.B. with all my love, November 1992."
He must have signed the book the next day
thinking it was hers, thinking she would
see it later and think of him, their pale bodies
riding the white page of the bed, as though it had been
his idea, as if he was the one who had given her
some kind of gift.

IT WAS GOOD TO GROW UP
WITH THE BOMB

Joe McCarthy, the Bay of Pigs,
a mushroom cloud our central metaphor.
Good to know the flash, echo, hiccup
and the long, slow sigh across the desert.
Good to see houses bowled over by wind like
crash-test dummies without seatbelts.

At sixteen I sat in a restaurant,
held to your talk of classes and teachers,
to skin silk under the angora sweater,
lost in the lecture you gave
the night before with your tongue in the
backseat of my mother's Ford. My surprise
at how much there was to learn.

The waitress brought more coffee. I thought
I saw you across the table in my future, married,
the children at summer camp and you steering me
toward the gift of your body
away from the desk where I wrote.
It was good to think of us living that long.

Good to hear sirens whine to life outside, notice
the air-raid tower across the road for the first time,
other patrons glancing, curious. There was nothing
we could do if missiles were coming – the world was
about to end and we would all die, had been
expecting to for years. This was it.

We looked at each other,
saw how the world was made in seven days, saw
the earth and oceans of the first day, and fish, and
birds, and animals; the garden and finally
the man and woman in it, and we thought
if it could be made and then taken apart,
it could be made again.

CONTROLLED BURN

It is spring and dry, snow
retreats to glaciers. Though clouds drift over
they refuse to spill on mountain backs.

I hike with her in the valley.

I'm so dumb you have to
bang me on the head
before I believe you want me;
you'd have to say something like . . .
"I want to fuck you blind," she says.
"Yeah, something like that," I say.

Deer tend fawns and push
into the forest, darkened at midday;
overabundant trees seem to say
no trespassing, this means you
foolish boy. Grow up.

Rangers light a fire on the mountain,
a controlled burn to keep timber
from torching itself should lightning
or a cigarette ignite it.

Wind shifts against forecasts,
the fire leaps over itself.
They water-bomb with helicopters,
heavy bees buzzing the slopes with
bellies full of chemical mist.

I lean out my window
to watch it glow, smoke a cigarette.
The tape in my head rewinds,
plays the conversation over and over.
This is the beginning of my life.

THE MOON CHANGES,
EVEN AS YOUR MIND

Then, God be bless'd, it is the blessed sun:
But sun it is not, when you say it is not;
And the moon changes, even as your mind.
What you will have it nam'd, even that it is;
And so it shall be so.

– Shakespeare,
The Taming of the Shrew, IV, v.

The sign hanging on the hotel door says:
Maid, Please Make Up This Room.

She stands before it, knowing
about the unmade bed,
the film of dead skin
and hair in the tub, white towels on the floor.
This is a day like others,
full ashtrays, bars of wrapped soap.

But today, she looks at the door
and says 'No, not this emptiness.
Not this time, not again.'
Cleaning up after another
one night on business or holiday stopover.
Is this life?

She makes up the room
differently with her mind
so that when she reverses the sign
the day changes, even as her thoughts resolve:
a man pushed up against the pillows,
a woman riding him as if crossing
a long desert on a horse, beads of sweat
down her naked back, her feet
coiled like snakes, restless in the hot, Mexican sun.
Two whose mouths are so full of each other,
they can not speak, or be disturbed.

SKATING

. . . crosses the blue line and
he's all alone . . .

And now I *am* interested in sports:
Olympic athletes on several televisions
push their bodies further than love or talk
would take them, exhausted
fall into the snow
at the finish line. Two women
jostle for space on the speed oval,
blades counting threats as arms
pendulum over the finish.

The late February snowstorm has transformed
this part of Canada into Japan, snowflakes
seemingly placed
in the centre of open cherry blossoms land
swift as our chance meeting.

Is it a coincidence
that a woman approached with
a bamboo umbrella?

Now, by the fire in a smokey pub
TV screens broadcasting Norway in
every corner, I want
to apologize for my guilty eyes that flit
to the hockey game, as to a summer skirt:
drawn to 'Canada vs. Finland'
in the way they are drawn
still
to you.

But I have learned not
to apologize, Love,
despite the absence
of your husband and my wife,
because being here is as good as this talk
interrupted as the line of drinkers by the bar stand
at patriotic attention and cheer
when the home team manages the impossible.

LONG DISTANCE

Late talks on the phone; we were
boys mumbling into tin cans
amazed at the sameness of our voices,
the way our lives travelled Euclidean paths.
Speaking of desire –
to dive into life like a wave
not sure about coming up for breath;
how a kite is nothing
without string.

How can I stand in the middle
of an October field, I said,
while the leaves around me discuss
their dead friends?
It's embarrassing, this redness,
the determination to *hang on.*

Should I curl like a cat into my wife,
telling how the day went, what was on sale?

My envy when you said you
drove away in a fury of fall rain
heading south with your window open.

It's as simple as this:
a man stands in an empty street
at six a.m. unable to return
home to the wife he loves.

Decision crackles in the air,
crisp as dry leaves
crumbled to nothing in a fist.

STORM

I would name a hurricane after you
the way you lash your tongue along the
brown hide of the planet, picking off
homes like buttons.

You are the kind of tornado
that plucks children from their mother's grasp
and whirls them halfway to Oz
before their eventual rest
in the crossed arms of a heron's nest
by the river.

You blow into my life,
disturb dust in all the corners
of my contentment so I
offer myself to a bird for safekeeping,
hide from searching fingers.
Your own bared flesh descends like clouds
filling my mountain valleys, wet with the energy
of earth and air colliding.

I could stand back from this feasting of weather,
hide myself in the dark root cellar.
If I stayed long enough you might pass over.

Instead I watch you coming.
Clouds gather around you in the distance,
shifting over landscape like a naked woman,
turning into white sheets on a used bed.

BREATH

A long transit ad on the number 28 shows
two lovers
taking each other's breath away.
Passion says
more than sugared mint,
sparking their tongues electric
on the smooth other of teeth.
They are surrounded by marble
and glow like a Picasso:
the blue period.

She looks determined, palm
under the back of his neck as if she were
holding a glass bowl.

He looks surprised;
he can't believe his luck.

They are beautiful
riding day and night over all
the city's bridges,
locked in the sweetness
of first falling.

The riders have been swaying,
long prairie grass shoulder to shoulder
but – in a moment of unbelievable synchronicity –

everyone turns to look at the photo-lovers
at the same time and are touched.

Throughout the day riders all over town
are approached by others
of startling beauty,
people they expected only to see
in movies or magazines,
and are kissed unexpectedly
with a passion that says
this will never end.

FLIGHT 3625:
VANCOUVER TO TORONTO

How easily we rise.
What was the world
is the black strip laid down
like a tongue across a field
that opens and widens,
loses its fences
and becomes the space
surrounded by houses –
entire lives in each,
dishes pile up in the sink,
the kid whines that her
favourite Saturday morning cartoon
has been pre-empted for PGA golf,
or any of the thousand
small bodies next door
moving in or out with groceries
or a lawnmower
until the plane banks
and the order of streets fades,
is divided by coastline,
the jagged, white emphasis of waves
bracketing the city.

I am holding no one close,
my own heart in shards waiting
to settle in one city or the other.
The seat next to me empty so I

stretch my legs and still
see out the window.
Far below, a gull arches
like a shooting star over the ocean.
Then there is a fishing boat,
its wake fanning out peacock-like
as the plane flies onward,
into the morning and over another city:
the suburbs on the delta kaleidoscope
around a centre, an open-pit mine
spirals into its core in steppes
and the great rafts of lumber, linked to make
long lines and circles, spells out
moaning ecstasy in Morse code
along the banks of the river.
Even the clear-cut forests
as we drift eastward away from town
make patchwork, intricate patterns we
move through too close to see how
the mazes guide us; designs
scar the earth like rose tattoos,
a lift to forty-thousand feet and sunrise.

CHESTERMAN'S BEACH

Low tide in moonlight, the beach
relaxes toward the lighthouse, broad
as a man's back in a Mapplethorpe photograph;
reflection of the moon between shoulders.

This place is plagued by ghosts,
the site of a battle
between tribes, the hollow *whop*
a skull makes
giving in to the weight of a club.

In the cabin I am sleepless, rise
from the bed leaving
the warmth of your body
spilled in dreams between sheets,
turn pale in fridge light when I
slip into the kitchen for a drink.

On the shelf, a book of Pat Lowther's poems
shirks among thrillers and murder mysteries,
a shy child in a class of hoodlums.

The wind is up and I sink into her words.
The room weathers the storm.
She speaks from her grave of pages
after the jealous husband shot her.

Bulbs blink and go out.

I strike a match that glows spirit-bright
in the room's blackness,
light a candle to read by:
a dead woman's poems, wind, and your breathing.

GARDENIA

Once in a life,
just once before you die,
to fall in love so completely
that you wish for death
when your husband's body
fails him and he leaves it –
so absolutely
the forty years after seem hushed,

the way this night is quiet.

Alone in a night garden
one bloom
white
as the moon on its deathbed,
against broom, cedar, and the Pacific:
a clear night, every star out
wet grass dries on my feet.

The scent echoes incense of
the corsage someone gave you
just before you died,
the way the moon reflects previous light.

Wonder at how in the midst
of missing you

someone else emerges whose heart petals I could
have plucked:
> *loves, loves me not.*

Those words shrouded
in a wash of new perfume.

I want to keep that pinned thing,
blossoming forever
in the dark fridge,
wet towels wrapped around the stem so its breath,
when I open the door,
fills the room
the way the memory of someone
surprises the mind.

GLASS EYE

An everlasting gobstopper
he pops in his mouth to clean.

"Don't tell my wife I'm showing you this."

Through it the world
kaleidoscopes, sun sparking, prismatic.
Blistered edges of the cat in the window.
I look at the coffee cups,
the cash register.

In my palm it rolls
like a marble, sparkling.
He looks at me with his good eye,
dark socket also aiming.

I want to hand it to him
but can't look away.
The eye has me
and there is nothing to do but gaze back
into its lake, blue sky,
the woman in the garden.

THE SKY THAT NIGHT

Last night a spent Russian rocket
tore open the sky
drawing blood: evening
bordelloed by sudden light. Wounds
like scratches on flesh
when an animal panics.

Its red glow cast over the city
and some said this was the miracle
they'd been waiting for:
the eclipse's opposite, the end times.

There is the story of a European colonizer
tied to a stake in South America,
saved by the luck
of a solar eclipse
he knew was coming.
"If you kill me," he said,
"I will take away the sun
and your world will grow cold."
As proof he said he would
darken the sky the next afternoon.

What did he think of
the night before,
hands crossed above,
notched high in the post?

Sometimes the sky
refuses to catch us
so we descend, exhausted from
the weight of just living.

Or clouds open
and light escapes behind the moon
describing thoughts of heaven.

Sometimes things go well.

A MAP OF THE WESTERN STATES

It happened that evening
just after the sun had set,
this child on the back porch
let the screen slam perfectly
like the code of the universe finally
being cracked
and everyone everywhere at last
was released beyond the thin
transparency you and I had felt
so many times
in the carpool on the way to
or from work; that
for some reason we *knew*
as the kid set down the bowl of milk
and called the cat,
we knew
just this once that we should
really have been living
in Mosca, Colorado
together all this time.

But I could be wrong about that.
It might be that we would have done better
in Pojoaque, New Mexico, or
Bear River City, Utah; maybe
Avila Beach, California.
Yeah, California, where the sun
takes the water off the tanned back
of a surfer
doing what he has dreamed of doing
since he was fifteen,
thinking about the girls around him
bikinied, cinematic like they're supposed to be,
the way the last wave curled just so,
him needling right through,
thinking how lucky he is, how he never
thought he would be so lucky.

JANE

*Jane Jones strips with a Siberian tiger named Quadesh but
has been prevented from using a flaming baton in the act.*

— Wire item

You know the scene I guess, the way the doors
close behind you cutting off natural light,
the coloured spots above the empty stage,
the brass poles,
the men
placed like desert shrubs
around their tables, beer, waiting,
the way the music starts
the men perk up, and Jane Jones
walks out onto the stage
spotted like a leopard in a bodysuit.
She throws a blanket in the corner,
cracks her whip and begins to dance
and move, this time without
her flaming baton
as she shifts her body toward
the eye-level men in the first row
whose looks nearly pop out
when Quadesh the tiger is released
down a ramp and comes straight for her
looking wary at first, nervous, as if the spotted leotard
was something he'd never seen before.

At least that's what some of the men
would speculate later if everything went wrong.

Imagine Jane catching a new look in Quadesh's eyes,
a message he need not speak
for her to fast peel off the suit,
banana-like, from the top down
until she is so naked and vulnerable
that it seems no harm should
rightfully come to someone like that.
Jane would look over the men
as if one might be Tarzan after all,
wishing his throaty, operatic call
would make the tiger stop
and run home in the other direction.

What if no one saves her and this time,
right in front of everybody,
he eats her, swallowing all the parts
and dreaming of a girl tiger he knew long ago,
how her fur shone like the dance of Shiva
in the desert as she walked across a plain,
or emerged from a clump of trees
and the noises they made when they mated,
she pushing up into him and he riding
the blanket of her back
bawling and purring
his voice spreading outward
as atoms of sound dance and fade and are born.

ON FIRST LOOKING OVER
CHAPMAN MOTORS

Another mall with a food store
going out of business,
the coffee shop, dentist and
chiropractor still attracting customers
in the cold November of market forces.

Another car dealership way out of town
so the only way to get there is to drive.

Turn off the radio and pull in
to look at the ancient Volvo sports car
with maniac grinning bumpers.

The day before there was the guy I hardly knew
breaking down and weeping in front of me
because he'd smashed his new Mustang GT
and I wanted to tell him to get a fucking life,
but instead allowed my body to separate
and for the gentle part to
wrap its wimpled arms around him:
'there, there.'

I kicked the tires and looked under the hood.
There was a motor.
Bob Chapman came out of his shack
and sized me up as if I had wheels.
The best I could do was,
"Does it have a radio?"

I thanked him for letting me look,
got back in my own humble wagon and drove.
A Hindi version of Beethoven's "Ode to Joy"
was breaking out of the speakers
and I scraped homeward
wishing for words I could sing.

LIFE ON MARS

The blizzard came that year,
not an onslaught, not wind from the mouths
of mountains or cold that would stop
life-sap in veins, just
snow, lots of it, tumbled from the sky
like a heavenly Greek pillow fight
and no winners until the car was covered –
only the aerial poking out of a drift.
In the morning I opened
the back door to a white wall
and thought some trickster
had boarded up the house with sugar-coated planks.
I dug all morning so my dog
could pee and still snow came down.
I thought I'd have to build
an ark, load up the pets.
For days after, the whole city shut down,
buses rested on their laurels, and former
prairie dwellers dug out their old snowshoes.

All anyone could do was wait.

The neighbour spent twelve hours
digging out his sidewalk
sculpting perfect right angles deep
as the Panama Canal although
there was nowhere to go once he got to the street.

His shovel made fruitless order out of chaos,
carved ditches sharp as canals on Mars
that suggest that once there was civil order there,
once there were streets and bright cities
chiselled into the bright red earth that was home
to a people not unlike us, antennaed
men and women who loved each other
in the warm beds of a Martian winter,
praying the world would never end.

FAITHFUL STREET

In my neighbourhood people
beat their children on the front lawn,
"Come'ere ya little bastard,"
wails and screams like
sirens in a rabbit's throat.
A woman from social services
arrives half an hour later escorted
by cops, their arms looped in hers
as if she's reluctant and they're taking her in.

Last night shouting woke me
from a dream of pineapple and I
pulled on sweatpants, a shirt,
stumbled barefoot across the wet lawn
like a prisoner, feet dripping with
dew and rotten plums. Two men
faced off in the street. On the sidewalk
a woman with a baby watched, calling at them
to "stop it, stop it, stop it, you're going to
kill each other." They were brothers and the woman
had belonged to both of them, the crying baby
anyone's guess. Two cruisers, all lights off,
whisked in from either side of the street,
like commandos on a night raid
then doused the feud with light; the woman and child
disappeared like hocus-pocus.

Across town someone sculpts
an epic lawn, combing each square inch
for quack grass and the plague of dandelion seeds
allowing no variation in colour and texture:
a field of perfect green.
Lilacs burst out of their shells and what happens
behind broad oak doors is a secret.
Daughters emerge in sunlight and
keep their heads down, sons tell the gym teacher
they fell down the stairs. The father
straightens his tie and walks to the car,
cologne masking last night's scotch,
and he drives down the road
while blossoms, like fragrant bombs,
detonate from the limbs of trees.

MINISTRY

In the office across the street
men make laws.

There is a woman there also.

Her office is a garden
watered daily. She wears her body
like a new suit.
Sometimes she comes in late, or
leaves early in a hurry to get home
simply to make love.

The men choose their words warily.
They are sparing also
about decor. Only a certificate or two
hang in their offices.
One might guess that it goes further:
when they bend over a page
you might think it was a soul
they were searching for
to fill their lives.

It would be better if the lawmakers
were silent for a while.

I watch the woman
cross the threshold into the corner office,
walk up in front of the man's desk
and place her hand on his forehead,
unable to believe what he has written.

Then the dark languages are hushed,
then the bright green order
comes down without annunciation.
I have been waiting for this.
I have waited a long time.

MIES VAN DER ROHE

Her desk is near the elevators
on the fortieth floor of an office tower
in one of the big cities of
the new world. Maybe it's New York,
or Chicago, or Toronto, but anyway
it's where she works, taking calls
and booking appointments for the boss.
She buys birthday presents for the wife,
talks to the travel agent.

In the rooms behind her
rows of people in front of computers,
occasionally look up and wonder
how to intensify their lives.

Mies van der Rohe designed his buildings
with heat vents near windows,
furniture pushed back,
not spoiling the effect he wanted from
the ground. Lights left on at night
make it seem, as the city sleeps,
that his tower glows from within.

At the end of the day
she shuts down the machine
and misreads the screen asking,
Do you really wish to exist?

There is no other question.

In her apartment she watches TV,
flipping channels as though one of the stations
might even now be broadcasting dreams.

The late movie is *2010*
which she settles on just as
Dave disappears into the monolith.
The last thing anyone hears him say is,
"Oh my God. It's full of stars."

ALBINO CROW

In the pet shop are African rats
with tails like eager thumbs, hairless mice
that shiver wood chips, and a room full
of yellow budgies, green macaws;
an Amazon parrot whose sense of decorum
won't let it get past a sideways "Hello."

The crow has feathers like white silk,
not Michelin radials. In the mean world
it would have been pecked to death by its brothers
but someone must have reached down,
spilled it like a puff of smoke from a magician's hat
into this studious cage.

I stand in front of the wire and reconsider
my biases: the woman who first insisted
I drink tequila when I wanted only beer.
I remember her face when we made love,
the determination with which
she disappeared into herself while we rocked together
on her feather bed – although it was she who
burst out laughing later saying I looked
like I couldn't believe I was really there.
I loved her more for that.
We warmed night the way
air is warmed in evening by hot stones.

Our hands, if there had been light, would have
made birds on the wall.
There are things that should not be spoken of.

She went on to live a difficult sort of life
in another closet of my mind.
The crow's insouciant pose conceals
an anxious gaze, ivory beak still as she
casts her deep, pink eye around the room.

THE MYTH OF SISYPHUS

Light through the darkened blinds:
this old hotel by the water. I falter
to the bathroom, the shower
clears dream-energy, cold
snaps like a fresh sheet on a line.
I take a long time shaving, idle out
along the sea wall.

In Stanley Park dancers
spin over squares of a giant chessboard,
someone calls commands as they lock
and release arms, whirling –
a kaleidoscope of yoked shirts and frills.

On the walkway a man in a housecoat trudges
as though on an endless hike,
feet in sandals. He looks like an old escapee –
moves across the beach, sheds the housecoat and plunges
into the February ocean to swim.

This is a good life: walking in the weekday sun
while the city hums work and drudgery.

Other days I have contemplated
methods of not living, imagined
gas in the oven, a fall from the height of a bridge.
I have climbed and let go.
What stopped me?

Further down another man hauls logs
up the beach. He works
nine to five to earn his welfare cheque.
At night the sea undoes his work.

Sisyphus had a boulder to push forever uphill.
He could have solved his problem
by licking each time he leaned into it.
The weather of his tongue
eroding the rock into a stone he could wear.

JUMPER

There was a woman climbing in the rigs,
scaling bridge girders like an expert,
proteins in her thin arms fuelled by a bird
fluttering in her mind, calling
higher, wanting out. At the top
she stood and held her arms
in a kind of triumph, a climber
summiting a tough peak.

Cops gathered and closed down
the bridge just after I crossed it.
Someone clambered after her and she
ran across the top with the confidence of a gymnast.

I saw her fall, catch a hip of metal,
swaying pendulous by her outstretched arms.
She pulled herself up to catch her breath.

An ambulance stood by,
paramedics beside it talking as though
they'd just missed the last subway.

There was a woman sitting
in the hive of the bridge, talking
and no one could get close.
Her mouth moved
letting her story out.

A STORY

Be patient and words will come.
Language, like a flock of swallows lifting
through the ceiling
has left the whole group. Some
are weeping and the woman
who has just told us the story
of her son, the brilliant-eyed child
who would stand on the bed
with his arms outstretched for a hug,
the boy who, when she finally came
would leap and draw her close
collapsing her with the weight
of his love, this woman stands
with clasped hands
as if they were aware of the emptiness
so often between them.
The child died.
It is up to me to break this silence
but there are no sounds in my mouth.
A small creature has burrowed
in the hollow of my throat
and nothing, at any rate, should be set free.
Not a single syllable will break into the room's silence
to perform in the feathered air.

CHICKADEE POEM

I can't quite picture the staircase
but see you stop on the way up,
a sandwich in your hand when you hear
a chirp trill beyond the buzz of fluorescent lights.
A switch clicks, erasure, the way a good idea
slips away if you consider it too long.
So you go back down and find the bird
packed tight as a feathery tumour
in the guts of the step.

You think for a minute
to figure out what to do with the sandwich,
abandon it in its institutional-strength plastic,
reach in and cup the chickadee in both hands
as you used to do with grasshoppers as a child
feeling their violin bows rosin
in your curled palms.
Back out the glass doors, open
and see the tiny black thumbtack
blink once before it flies.

You go up to your office and
write a few lines. Teach a class,
stop in at the library.
Come back and look at letters
too obedient on the page.

"Nah," you say to yourself. "This is not the day
for a chickadee poem." You crumple
the paper but hold it
before tossing it in the wastebasket,
see a *dee*, and a *dee*, and a *dee* on the foolscap,
paper wings bent in your stalling hand.

SAILING

It is raining
the way it rains here – the city
washed away, brick buildings
tumble into the Pacific,
a cat clings to a lamppost.

The dead go on.
Tourists from the States
shop with oversized Eddie Bauer bags.
Does it matter
the sidewalk under their feet
is not what it seems?

What I was just wondering
is gone, carried away in a thought current.

Today I cannot stand
the silence between us,
the erasure of what is.

I remember your face and mine
melting on a hot afternoon
and the flood
when you lifted the water under my eye
with your tongue.

From here I can see
the brigantine *Spirit of Chemainus*
lift from the inner harbour,
the spar a cross
against a greying sea.

And there is a child
bent into the gutter
playing with the bottom of a Styrofoam cup:
a boat so small and simple
I could sail away in it.

THE CREATION OF ADAM

On the spring sidewalk the boy
is drawing God,
getting the long white hair flowing
in the right direction,
mixing two kinds of chalk
to get the colour of the robe right.

He's turned the Sistine Chapel
on its head, even put
jagged lines where the paint cracked
a hundred years after Michelangelo's death.

Then he draws Adam,
reluctantly reaching up
to God's accusing finger.
Stretch as he will,
God cannot touch him.

A few people have stopped to watch
and when he wants to draw under their feet
he levitates them.

I bring the kid home with me
and set him to work in the kitchen.

"Do something Italian-pastoral," I tell him,
and he starts drawing on the west side,
beginning at the window and working out.

In half an hour the wide wall
has disappeared.
He's put a bean field
in the distance where my neighbourhood used to be,
and a garden with tomatoes, basil, and a grapevine
up close to the kitchen.
Even better, he's made it late summer
so the fruit is ripe,
painted a wooden table
covered with homemade wine and with cheese.

"Don't stop now," I say,
"I'll be back;"
and when I return in an hour
there's someone making pesto
by the stove, grinding basil and garlic
so the room stinks with edible love.

In my daughter's room I find a manger
surrounded by farm animals,
sheep nudging me for grain
as I look down on her
glowing so brightly
I fear she'll set the straw on fire.

Leaving the baby with admirers,
my wife takes my hand and leads
to where the bedroom used to be.
Our clothes are erased,
we are standing in a garden
by a bed of woolly thyme,
and I'm thinking of the artist,
how much I must owe him,
when she pulls me down
under the tree of knowledge
and the last thing I hear is her voice:
"He's good, really good."

FISHING WITH THE BOY

My father squeezes the fuel bulb the same way his doctor
pumps the gauge to check his blood pressure,
primes gas into the motor before he puts his foot on it
and pulls the cord. The Johnson six-horse coughs to life
as if emerging from a long and difficult sleep.
He loosens the tie from the dock and steers the boat
toward the far side of the lake.

I sit backwards on the bow seat, watching him in the stern,
backlit by sunrise and a cloud of whirling mosquitoes.
He twists the throttle and his windbreaker flaps
in the breeze our speed makes across the still basin.
My hand trails in water. He doesn't know I'm testing myself,
conquering a fear of pike hungry
from a winter under the ice – *these fish will*
devour any part of a small boy.

He lifts his knee against the tiller to free his hands,
and pours coffee into the lid of the thermos.
The fishing rods bob out the back so from a distance
the boat is a waterbug going backwards.
He is taking us to the deepest part of the lake,
"Where the big ones are," he says, the pit of water
that hides the wildest water beasts, biggest teeth.

He slows the boat, stops, and my fingers sink
down deeper toward the abyss, tempting creatures
to rise from the bottom, my flesh irresistible.
My father looks at me frozen against life jackets.
He smiles but says nothing. He is happy.
There is nowhere he would rather be,
fishing with the boy he thinks he once was.
He lights a cigar and smokes,
takes out his tackle box to bait my line.
I will my hand to stay where it is, the gunnel
resting in my armpit like a crutch. Inside I'm screaming,
every spark of light on the surface a fish cruising for blood.

STAR

My father stands at the bottom of the stairs. I am crying
for my mother, lost
in the frozen foods section of Safeway.
Having found the gift of an afternoon alone –
my father free for the day from his usual labours
at the department store downtown –
it was all she could think of to do, go shopping for groceries
alone.

Today is the first day in kindergarten
that the teacher has given me a star for colouring;
most of the wax is inside the lines
and Ms. Funk has pronounced it good, although
the star is red, not gold, and I know
there is a message in this.

I stand on the upper landing
not knowing what it is to work everyday,
stay late wondering
how his store compares to others in the country,
waiting for the bosses to fly in from Toronto
to offer praise or criticism. The way that
he's beginning a life of work that will stop him
from saying "I love you."
I know only that he is not my mother, not the one
who led me by the hand my first day of school,
not the one to give this badge of honour to.

I pick under one of the star's bright points and peel it
from the page, like plucking wings from a fly.

My father below
has no idea what the problem is, no way to ask.
So he stands, looking up like someone
gazing at the night sky,
holding the rail tight.

THE SEVEN WONDERS OF
THE ANCIENT WORLD

*What do you do when your imaginary playmate
makes friends better than you do?*
> – Allucquere Rosanne Stone,
> "Violation and Virtuality"

Close the box lid and it's
a tunnel with no way out,
just dark where we can write with
crayons on the wall
not thinking anything we're marking down
until we open the flap again
to see what we said.
My parents used this
for clothes when we moved.

It's probably like being born
when you push toward the light
and squirm out headfirst.
You gotta go headfirst.
It's the rule.
Come in then but not for long.
Normally, you need to know the password.

This is Jerry. He has the final word
about whether you're in the club.
Say "Hello Jerry." Say it.

He stole these cigarettes
from my mom and if you're ordained
to the order of the gyroscope,
you can have one.
Jerry does what I tell him.
He can help you with school if you're in.
Jerry knows about integers,
he knows the date
Cartier discovered the St. Lawrence,
he knows the speed of light,
and the seven wonders of the ancient world.
He knows Steve's brother and Paula
didn't really do it like Steve says.
He knows the thoughts of horses
pretending to be stupid in the fields,
he knows the language
fish use to warn about hooks,
and he knows what you said about me
to Karen Deitz after school yesterday,
which is why, I'm afraid,
you're going to have to go through
the initiation.

THE GREEN-EYED MONSTER

In all the photos he looks
innocent as a child-saint,
blond hair curling against white
blankets in the crib, then flat on the
squarish head after haircuts.

"That one, oh he wouldn't hurt a fly."

Even the picture of him holding up
a string of trout, blood and the
ooze of life dripping from their curled tails, even
there his smile is part grimace. You'd guess
that the father made him do it,
the death of those creatures
was someone else's will.

Still, the parents called him the
green-eyed monster, those times he
wouldn't eat his beets or was caught
red-handed, reading C.S. Lewis
with a flashlight under sheets.

He could say he was beaten. That the father,
enraged by the gin that flowed
through his befuddled veins, held him up
by one arm and stripped down
the thin, flannel pajamas that a hundred
Tasmanian Devils watched him from.

True or not he could tell how the small
naked bottom was paddled
with a flat hand that fell on the skin over
and over like a tool for tenderizing meat,
the wedding ring sparking
in the glint of the nightlight and cutting
into flesh, so finally the blood made him stop.

What if the boy described the mother
sitting on his bed years later,
speaking the way a parishioner
confesses to a priest, saying she would
leave that haunted place if she could.

He could invent a sister
growing thinner and thinner as each night
after dinner she bent over the toilet
to choke the sap of food out, release of poison.

That monster, that green-eyed boy,
they had no idea how dangerous he could be.

They didn't know that inside was a fiend, one who
imagined the smell of a pillow heated by weeping, the
sound of the sister's muffled cries in the dark.
What if he spoke these things as truth,
waved them in the streets like evidence at a trial?

LOMBARD STREET

He says yes to the long drive knowing
there will be fights with the brother,
threats from the father,
the mother's silence and bad navigation
through complex American freeways.

Yes to Alcatraz, trolley cars,
someone he wishes he could be momentarily
skateboarding down a steep incline
toward the low and distant bay,
Chinatown, and Fisherman's Wharf.
Yes to dinner at the Hilton
with its palate-cleansing sorbets between courses.

Yes to Lombard Street, the most
twisted street in the world,
the family car climbing and
this small boy outlined in the rear window,
his balloon an empty word bubble in the frame –
some cartoon character who forgot
what he was about to say.

Yes to the evening drive
across the Golden Gate Bridge,
as the city closes its slow eyes.
Yes to the next day and drive home again,
to the next year when his voice broke,
and to first sex sweet in the attic of the cabin.

Yes to doing it again in the morning,
then to the few women in his life
who taught him what he knows.
Yes to the birth of his child,
to the house and jewelled yard around it.
Yes to the dog.

And now he's well into it,
there's no turning back.
Around another hairpin climbing steadily
beyond the silence surrounding
the dog's inevitable end,
so yes even to the death of his parents and
yes to being there each time.
Yes to all the routes that sent him
corkscrewing forever up like an aria.
Yes to watching his daughter
back the car down the driveway
graduating highschool. Then yes to
old age and to senior's discounts at Sears.
Yes to memory and forgetting,
the decline of his body,
to those who check on him on weekends,
and to the someone who pushes him
out to the park in a wheelchair.
Yes to light and dark and closing,
and Lombard Street's hedges and red bougainvillaea.

SWITCHBACK

We're packing the tent when the man jogs by, eyes
wide like a chased deer: "Have you seen
a girl in a blue dress?" holds his hand out as though bouncing
a basketball, "She's *this* big."

The lake rolls its tongue along the shore
as though it might be hiding something.
I check the surface for ripples smoothed over.

Driving out of Osoyoos, up the eastern slope with
a car full of borrowed children, I check the mirror for
a girl in a blue dress but she is not among them.

Looking down around another hairpin I step on it and rise.
In the valley I see something the colour of sky
on horseback, riding the wild desert toward freedom.

Over my shoulder another child is reflected in memory:
my friends' son who never made it to this side of the world,
turned back stillborn. I could give
one of these kids to the sunken parents.

It's so easy to get away.

Somewhere in that field of beige below
the girl in the blue dress waits for her father,
his quick anger melting in relief when he
finally sees her, standing transfixed by horses.

I check the mirror again, driving. The children
are making up stories as if this is
just another day to live through, and the
switchbacks, palm up, offer us to the sky.

LAST JUDGEMENT
Daniele de Volterra (1509 – 1566)

In the mirror he sees the skin that holds him together,
turns his broad back toward the candlelight, then
faces himself again: the bulge of fat around his middle
that won't go away, wisps of black hair
around the navel and lower, the troubling
net of fuzz – a sudden forest on a plain.
The slouching penis like the top half of a worm,
the other part stuffed inside him. There's the leather
coin purse hanging there too, and long white legs falling away.

He is known as *Il Braghetone*, "the breeches maker".

For a year his broad strokes of colour have been
washing over his mentor's art, covering exposed genitalia
in Michelangelo's "Last Judgement" with
trousers and draperies, on Papal orders.

This is intimate work. All day high in the arches
of the Sistine Chapel he circles anatomy, moves in close
with his brushes, touches the bristles to a breast, the shaft
of a penis, strokes the crease of a vulva.

At night he dreams an orgy of body parts descending,
drowns in the erotic. Walking the streets he sees
only the lines of bodies beneath clothes,
as if he were responsible for this scene too,
with his paints expelling all citizens from Eden.

In the middle of the ceiling is St. Bartholomew, the last
to remain unveiled. De Volterra readies his brush.

In the tradition of martyrs who carry their mutilated parts,
St. Bartholomew holds his entire skin in his left hand.
He was flayed alive and Michelangelo painted his own face
on the limp and sagging covering; a new Bartholomew,
naked and glorious, rising whole from his former body.

PORTRAIT OF A CHILD WITH FEVER

All morning the child leans
into pillows on the couch,
her mouth half-open, eyes
rolling into her head
as unconsciousness gains a foothold
in the tussle she's having with it.
Inside her body there's a full-scale
war going on, a guerilla campaign,
saboteurs in black-face
blowing up bridges at night.

Her skin is red with fever-heat.
She looks angry, like the mad
pig in the cartoon she watches,
fists clenched, straight legs
bouncing off the ground
and steam whistles
hooting out his ears.

She won't even drink water, preferring
to dip into the dream pond
she swims in as the father dabs a cool cloth
on her forehead. At what point does he
wrap her in the quilt and rush to the hospital,
admit that her antibodies are losing?

She shrugs him off as if he were an insect,
lifts up out of herself and floats toward the screen.

She enters that world of colour.
A turtle walks a field of bright pixels.

DRINKING SONG

Later, Terence refills my wine glass
with the sixteen-year-old scotch
he's been saving; I pour it down my throat
smooth as holy water and spin away from the kitchen,
drifting from talk and the Christmas tree.

Language sags in my mouth,
wet laundry pinned to a line.

The children are warring. They slash – vicious Huns
with cardboard tubes from wrapping paper.
I stumble onto the battlefield, am given
a weapon – an errant knight
heavy in armour, I will defend the honour
of the kingdom.

From the floor, I am a sudden landscape.
Horses gallop across the plain and
swords unfurl themselves in a fury,
carving up the country. My three-year-old
lops off my head as I struggle to rise.

Later, my wife heaves me into the back seat,
drives us home. I hold my daughter's hand
as the car swims through the blurred city.

When I emerge from sleep at four a.m. I am
adult again, filled with guilt
and the weight of drinking.

I stare at the ceiling, cringe
at thoughts that float onto the screen:
a cigarette butted in a teacup, pissing
on the neighbour's whitewalls,
a woman on the porch swearing she'll
never speak to me again while my eyes
make doubles of the stars and the night
turns on its great wheels.

FACE

She'll soon give up the afternoon nap
but for now she sleeps.

The face on the lawn is a sponge
for dipping in paint then on paper,
its crescent-smile never ending.
It does not mind its abandonment,
that she tossed it
from the summer deck.

I am surrounded by
dolls whose eyes close in sleep
but whose dimples never disappear,
and bears, zebras, and dragons.

I have shaken my daughter awake
certain she'd stopped breathing,
have left work early knowing
the house was burning down.
These days I am ill at ease
in my contentment, waiting
for tragedies that never play out.

While she sleeps, I roam the house
listening for the cries
that tell me she's still living.

I pick up small plastic people
trapped for months under the sofa
wanting to tell them grief
is the other side
of the pleasure their faces speak of.
They never argue.

They think I'm a gas.

THE GOLDEN PHEASANT

At the children's zoo in Stanley Park
I sit my daughter on my lap and ride
the miniature train through the forest,
knees jutting out like a grasshopper's,
trying not to look foolish
when the steam whistle blows.

And here is my girl with farm animals:
she punches her hand into a sheep's coat
and the whole of it disappears. The way water
can take off an arm.

At the back of the barn, the golden pheasant
graces us with his presence; his metallic cap and
neck ring are not right for this era. He belongs
in a fairy tale where a witch has cast a spell
on a just-crowned king.

She is more impressed by black squirrels,
ducks that beg for popcorn.
As I carry her back to the car she falls asleep
to my feet's rhythm.

I think about the bird, the golden eggs of legend.
I never asked for happily ever after,
just the sharp rise and fall of living, days
when I have wanted to walk into the ocean
and forget how to swim, and days when a child
trusts herself to sleep in my arms,
waking with questions, wanting
to know the whole story.

THE TYNDALL EFFECT

My brother drives for an hour and a half
to meet me for lunch, says, "Come for dinner at my house,"
offers to take me there and back before midnight.
He'll make the return trip again under late stars
and get home in time for work.

His wife has left him but is there for dinner,
pulling roasted meat out of the oven that is now
his. The children climb me like a
playground they remember visiting once
and I pluck shreds of real peach
from yogurt to keep it pure.

Phone calls this past year
rolled over on his bill like an odometer –
talking and talking until I was nearly asleep sometimes,
his heart rising and falling as he spoke,
weeping into his cellphone and then falling back
into the shell of his protected self: "I'd better let you go."

We become our parents. Drowsy with wine
I let the seat slip back and he drives us out of the city
into the night. He doesn't know what to do with
her sometimes gentleness now that rings have been returned.
She bought a house down the street.
There are the things she said in the months after they split,
they were sorting out possessions and he asked
about the photo albums, pictures of them together, looking

happy. She would have scissored him
out of the frame in every one then.

May, but snow starts falling just out of town. I remember
the Tyndall effect from high-school science, the way
light finds itself suspended against particles
that throw themselves in its way:
dust in kitchen sun, smoke
in the angles of the projector showing movies
of Fred and Ginger dancing. This snow
in the light of headlights.

He is still in love; there is longing for the life
he wanted to have, the desire to erase
this past year from memory, take up with her again
as if he'd spent no time alone,
walking through the empty rooms of that big house
after he hung up the phone, finding memory
in the beds of his only-weekends son and daughter.

He drops me off at midnight and I ask him to stay,
get up early and go back. But he is used to
driving for miles in blizzards of his invention.

Perhaps he will keep talking as he drives,
as if I was still there to listen. My shadow-self
will navigate, lean over as the wipers haul,
will say he loves him.

I wish I could say this trip at night on an icy highway –
the large and falling snow, the wall of white
more sudden in high beams
is not a metaphor for what life has become. But I have dined
in his splintered home, have heard theories and confessions.
There is a route here somewhere but I can't see it.

BLUE HIMALAYAN POPPIES

The stems, in their happiness, wave goodbye,
a dart-pattern of spear grass caught
against the black dog's ankle.
Seeds and their smallness; the way they
ride toward the future always.
Such hope makes unlikely light
from the most distant stars possible.
Later in the day they'll drop
into the warm earth.
I never guessed you
would have crossed some great distance
to settle everywhere
in my arms.

How was I to know
this, briefly, like the touch
of smallest fingers, after
a long winter and the
Chinese New Year. End
of the Year of the Dog,
beginning of the Year
of the Pig. Does it matter?
Maybe not, except summer now,
full of your small self on my shoulders
and how the sun
catches in sea-spray,
rocks below and the edge moving
further off.

This morning
I read the poems my friend sent:
postmarks from Izmir and Parma.
Sometimes I think this house,
the mortgage – my god there's a
station wagon in the driveway –
even you, sometimes I think, even you . . .
I am jealous of languages I don't understand,
mosques with roofs like round fruit.
The seeds of fruit that can't grow
unless a bird digests them,
sprouted like second spines.
The planet revolves under our feet,
around the sun, around
the centre of the centre,
as in the living room
I hold you tight and spin
to the sound of Billie Holiday.

Most seeds are lifted by wind.
This afternoon I blew
white dandelions across the yard.
There are days meant for us
when the light is trying to tell us something.
Even the blue Himalayan poppy,
which blooms once perfectly before dying,
is showing off.
I talk in your mouth

and you open bird-like
to swallow words.
This is my pleasure.
You like round ones best:
igloo, overalls, loop, moon, shoe.
There is nothing in this milky world
as small as your breath.

Do you know coconuts
migrate by water to new beaches?
They collapse on the dunes after
all that time of waves
passing them hand to hand.
To live in a place like this you must first
imagine it.
Already I am sad for anything
you missed while you were here.
But I walk with you until you sleep.
Somewhere is a beach, a palm
and high in its branches a bird,
red feathers declaring
I am here.

ACKNOWLEDGEMENTS

This book involves a mash of influences and inspirations for which I would like to particularly thank Hana Ruzesky-Bashford, Lucy Bashford, John Harley, Laurel Bernard, Lee Goreas, Laura Anderson, Jennifer McMackon, Terence Young, Pierre McKenzie, Janice MacCatchen, Donnato Lemmo, Stacey Engles, Sarah Nelems, Nap and Shirley Ruzesky, Scott Ruzesky, Sherrie and Gord Lewis, Richard Lemm, Lesley Anne Bourne, Marlene Cookshaw, Michael Kenyon, Sharon Thesen, Helene Demers, Chuck Lemery and Cody.

Special thanks to PK Page, Don Coles, John Lent and Steven Heighton for their readings. I'm especially grateful to Patricia Young, my steadfast editor. Finally, a big thanks to Silas White at Nightwood Editions for shepherding the book through the press swiftly and thoughtfully.

I am obliged to the editors of the following magazines and anthologies in which several of these poems first appeared:

The Antigonish Review, Arc, The Art Tree, Border Crossings, Canadian Forum, Descant, Event, The Fiddlehead, Grain, Intersections: Poetry and Fiction from the Banff Centre for the Arts, The Literary Review of Canada, New Canadian Poetry, The New Quarterly, Pottersfield Portfolio, Prism International, Queen's Quarterly, The Queen Street Quarterly, The Underground Review, Vintage 1999 and *Vintage 2000.*

A chapbook also called *Blue Himalayan Poppies* was published by the Hawthorne Society, Victoria BC, 1995. Thanks Charles, wherever you are, and Rhonda.

"The Myth of Sisyphus" is John Harley's idea. The information in "Last Judgement" is drawn from Stephen Jay Gould's essay, "Layering," in *The Sciences* (March/April 1999).

"Gardenia" is in memory of Diana Regester; "Long Distance" is for Steven Heighton; "It Was Good to Grow Up with the Bomb" is for Sarah Nelems; "A Story" is for Jennie Thomas; "Chickadee Poem" is for Sharon Thesen; "Blue Himalayan Poppies" is for Hana.

Thanks to the Leighton Colony at the Banff Centre for the Arts where some of these poems were written.

Thanks to the Canada Council for the Arts for financial support.